BINGE CONTROL:
A Compact Recovery Guide

Cynthia M. Bulik, PhD, FAED

Copyright © 2015 Cynthia M. Bulik

All rights reserved.

ISBN-13: 978-1505861761

DEDICATION

To the wonderful advocates who have taught me so much about using your voice to change the world.

DISCLAIMER

All matters regarding your health require medical consultation. This handbook reflects my decades of experience as a psychologist and director of eating disorders treatment and research programs. It is neither intended nor designed to replace the opinions of your health care professional.

CONTENTS

	Introduction	i
1	What is BED?	1
2	Who Suffers from BED?	5
3	Why Me? What Causes BED?	8
4	BED and Weight Stigma	11
5	Psychological Treatments for BED	14
6	Medication Treatments for BED	18
	Closing Remarks	21
	Appendix: Where to Find Help and Support	22

ACKNOWLEDGMENTS

I am grateful to Emily Bulik-Sullivan, Natalie Bulik-Sullivan, Susan Kleiman, and Lizabeth Wesely-Casella for editorial and creative assistance and to Richard Curtis for his ongoing support of my work. Thanks also to Chevese Turner for ongoing inspiration.
Cover art by Max Englund and photo by Ulf Sirborn.

INTRODUCTION

Binge-eating disorder, or BED, is the most common eating disorder. It affects men, women, boys, and girls. It cuts across race and ethnicity, income levels, sexual orientation, and age. Although first recognized as an official disorder in 2013, it has been around for a long time, and we know quite a bit about it. This handbook is a compact guide to understanding BED and a companion to my book *Crave: Why You Binge Eat and How to Stop*. It is designed to help people who have BED better understand their condition and their treatment options and to help family members and friends of individuals with BED provide understanding and support to their loved ones during recovery. The most important message in this handbook is that **BED is treatable**. Many effective therapies and medications exist. The goal is to know what is available and to find the treatment or combination of treatments that work best for you.

1 WHAT IS BED?

I've been doing this for years but I never knew it had a name. I just thought I had a willpower problem. Food was my Achilles' heel. My family doctor kept telling me to lose weight, but every time he did, I just went home and almost in defiance, ate more—sometimes a whole family-size bag of chips—and that was just the start of it. I'm not sure how I thought that eating would get back at him for implying I was fat...the only person I was hurting was myself. But once I started eating, I couldn't put the brakes on.
— Chuck, diagnosed with BED at age 53

Binge-eating disorder, or BED, is the most common eating disorder. Around 4.2 million women and 2.3 million men in the United States suffer from BED. In 2013, for the first time, the American Psychiatric Association recognized BED as an official eating disorder in their catalog of mental illnesses, the *Diagnostic and Statistical Manual of Mental Disorders Fifth Edition* (DSM-5). It took quite some time for this recognition to come about even though we have been doing research on the syndrome for decades. At long last, the disorder that has been torturing so many people for so long has a name. Here's what BED looks like.

Recurrent binge eating. Officially, this means eating, in a discrete period of time, an amount of food that is definitely larger than most people would eat during a similar period of time and under similar circumstances, *coupled with a sense of loss of control over eating*. To the person with BED, it may feel like a craving or an intense urge to eat. The pressure mounts and only food can satisfy the urge. Sometimes a binge happens in response to stress, anxiety, depression, or anger (negative emotions). Sometimes it happens in response to positive emotions. Sometimes it seems to come out of the blue. For many, it transitions to habit, and they may no longer be able to pinpoint the triggers.

Distress. Even though there may be fleeting pleasure as an individual starts the binge episode and enters the *binge zone*, fundamentally, binge eating causes distress. The distress may be associated with guilt, shame, or embarrassment about losing control, about weight gain, or about the financial toll of BED.

Frequency. Although any amount of binge eating can be distressing, the official diagnosis is made when an individual engages in binge eating on average once a week for a period of three months or more.

The binge zone. People with BED use different language to explain the lure of binge eating. Calming, numbing, dissociating, escaping, relaxing...these are all terms that are used to describe what I call the *binge zone*. As the pressure to binge mounts, people with BED become more driven, anxious, and uncomfortable. They develop a sense of being compelled to eat. They may arrange their environment in such as way as not to be interrupted and not to be discovered. Once they have done so, and they take that first bite, they enter the *binge zone*. A sense of relief washes over them. The first bites might be frenzied or slow, but most people say that they do experience the smell, sight, and texture of food in the beginning stages of a binge. Then things become blurry and nondescript and the behavior just becomes rote hand-to-mouth until they are uncomfortably full or get interrupted in some way. The *binge zone* gives them a temporary break from whatever they are trying to escape. Unfortunately, it is only temporary, as the guilt and disgust rush back in as they exit the zone and become aware of what they have done. The lure of the zone is what keeps BED alive in much the same way that the thought of the next drink or the next fix maintains alcohol or drug abuse.

Weight. Body weight or body mass index (BMI) is not part of the diagnostic criteria for BED. However, for many individuals with BED, weight is an issue, and it may have been a central issue throughout most of their lives. BED strikes individuals of any body shape and size. Many people with BED claim that extreme diets and desperate attempts to control their weight in the past contributed to the development of their BED. We'll discuss this more in Chapter 4. However, at this point, it is critical to acknowledge that a thin person, a normal-weight person, and an overweight person can all suffer from BED.

Associated features. Beyond the diagnostic criteria, other hallmarks of BED exist. Many argue that BED is as much a dieting disorder as it is a "binge-eating" disorder and clarify that many people with BED develop cycles of binge eating and dieting in a futile chase after permanent weight loss. Depression, anxiety, and substance abuse commonly co-occur with BED. Pervasive dissatisfaction with weight and shape can fuel the cyclic chase for weight control.

BED is not bulimia nervosa. BED should not be confused with bulimia nervosa. In bulimia, binge eating is coupled with regular compensatory ("purging") behaviors (such as self-induced vomiting, laxative use, extreme exercise, etc.). Although people with BED may occasionally engage in compensatory behaviors, they do not do so regularly, as in bulimia nervosa.

Pamela

On the outside, Pamela is a highly successful woman. She is competent...almost to a fault. On most days she is cheerful, even when it is an effort. She is obliging. She is a genuine friend. She'll bend over backwards for you. She laughs heartily. She puts everyone else's needs before hers. In fact, she's not even sure what her needs are. She is dependable; the one that others rely on. She can multitask and keep many balls in the air. She is always there for her parents and for her kids. She says she's not resentful when her siblings or her husband assume that she'll take care of everything.

People compliment her on all she does, but inside Pamela never feels like she does enough or does things well enough. If she does nine things perfectly and one thing less than perfectly, she only remembers the one thing that wasn't up to her standards. She ruminates over mistakes and second-guesses herself constantly.

Occasionally, Pamela vacillates between self-doubt and a vague sense of superiority, but the self-doubt wins because she feels unworthy of the positive self-esteem.

The chatter that goes on in her head doesn't always match her outward demeanor. Pamela might be fuming on the inside, but only partially be aware of it. She's not sure if she deserves to be angry, but she is nonetheless furious inside. She desperately wants someone to recognize all that she is doing without having to ask for that recognition. But if someone does praise her, it is difficult for her to take the compliment.

She is someone whom others rely on, except on those few days when she doesn't make it into work. She'll blame a migraine or "woman troubles," but the truth is that she was unable to recover from the binge hangover that left her raw and unable to put her mask back on in time to go to work.

What Pamela feels on the inside contrasts with what we see on the outside. When the shades are pulled after she comes home from work, or after the rest of the family goes to bed, the mask of competency is removed. She is exhausted from juggling the needs of others. She is deeply hungry from punishing herself for the previous night's binge by skipping breakfast and lunch. She feels entitled to the only thing that will fill the emptiness, suppress the anger, and feed the part of her that believes she deserves some pleasure. Food temporarily quells the emotional tempest inside, but does nothing to sort through the jumbled and indistinguishable, but powerful, feelings that rage inside her. Being in the binge zone gives her a moment of peace, of numbness, of calm. But the back end of the binge always leaves a swath of guilt, shame, and hopelessness that the cycle will just continue.

Pamela desperately wanted to change but did not know where to turn. She couldn't see the way out. She didn't want to stay in the cycle; she just needed a guide to help her balance other-care with self-care, to sort through and express emotions, and to find ways of addressing them in effective ways that did not involve food. She found help with both cognitive behavioral therapy and interpersonal therapy—each providing her with unique tools to deal with her BED. She got her binges under control. Equally importantly, her treatment allowed what she was feeling on the inside to match what others saw on the outside. She is binge free, she is still genuine, and she still has a hearty laugh. But rather than eating to solve every problem, now, when she's tired, she sleeps; when she's sad, she cries; when she's hungry, she eats, and she feels OK about it. She will still bend over backwards for you, but in her words, now she can tell you if you "piss her off", and she never misses her monthly massage.

2 WHO SUFFERS FROM BED?

BED does not discriminate on any dimension. It is promiscuous and will take root wherever it can. For some, it might be a transient experience; for others, it can persist for decades.

Age. Although the peak age that the disorder hits is in the late twenties, countless patients tell me that the roots of their binge eating reach back as far as they can remember. Since it is a little harder for children to tell us how much they are eating, and since their parents typically control their access to food, we often refer to the phenomenon of "loss of control eating" in children. Telltale signs of loss of control eating in children include: eating when stressed or emotional; mindless eating; not seeming to know when they are full; fast eating; eating alone; weight gain; hiding food or food wrappers; and anger or frustration when unable to eat. It is important to recognize that young children sometimes have huge appetites because they have high activity levels and they are growing—so just because they are eating a lot doesn't mean they have BED. But if enough of these signs are present, then it might be wise to seek a professional assessment.

College is also a peak time for the emergence of BED. For many, the transition from home to the cafeteria style dining, coupled with the stresses of college, can uncover difficulties with knowing how and when to stop eating. Many social events in college are built around (often unhealthy) food and alcohol, which can contribute to eating gone awry. Irregular meal times and lack of sleep also play a role in bodies losing their ability to know when they are full.

The majority of people with BED are adults. For some, it started in childhood and persisted. Others experience their first symptoms in adulthood. Pregnancy can also be a high-risk period for the development of BED. You don't grow out of BED. Just because a person is in her or his 60s, 70s, or beyond does not mean that BED is any less likely. Many of the later life challenges and transitions that we face like retirement or loss of a spouse or loved one can be powerful triggers for binge eating.

Sex. Men, women, boys, and girls all suffer from BED. They may talk about it differently and use different words to describe their experience, but they all suffer. Part of the problem is that binge eating causes shame for so many people. Those of us in the eating disorders profession look forward to the day when it is as easy for people to say, "I have BED" as it is to say, "I have allergies." The problem is that mental illness is fraught with stigma and shame, and eating disorders have a double dose of shame on top. Women are more likely to say that they feel like they lose control over their eating. For men, it is a little more comfortable to say they feel like they can't stop eating. How we ask questions about binge eating affects the answers we get. Whether someone identifies with BED, compulsive eating, food addiction, or emotional eating, doesn't matter. The important thing is that they recognize the problem and they get appropriate help.

Race and ethnicity. Individuals who are White, African-American, Latino, Asian, Native American, Pacific Islander, and other races and ethnicities all suffer from BED. A large study by the World Health Organization documented BED in 12 countries from Ireland to Brazil and everywhere in between. In the United States, several studies have documented even higher rates of BED among African American and Latino populations than in Whites. Stress associated with immigration and acculturation can be a strong trigger for Latino individuals. Many patients discuss being stuck between two cultures and torn between the food of their new country and the food traditions of the country they came from. Challenges finding culturally appropriate and affordable health care can delay seeking treatment and allow BED to become more serious.

Size. This point deserves repetition. BED does not discriminate on the basis of size. Although many people with BED are overweight, thin people, medium-sized people, and large people can and do suffer from BED. In some ways it is easier for thin or medium-sized people to have their BED go undetected. If an overweight person goes to her or his physician for a check-up, if lucky, the physician will ask about eating habits. Unfortunately, more often than not, the physician will recommend weight loss without asking about eating habits. However, people in the normal weight range are less likely to evoke questions about eating habits from their physician. Detection is one of the very important reasons why we need to raise awareness about BED and destigmatize the illness.

Income. Once again, BED does not care how much money you make. The disorder pops up across the income spectrum from the highest echelons to individuals on public assistance. The effect of poverty on BED is understudied, but the relatively cheap price of high-fat, high-sugar foods no doubt contributes to the development of BED. Importantly, BED costs money. Just like any addiction, fueling the urge to eat is not cheap. Many patients report serious financial consequences of BED.

Marisa

Marisa entered the United States at age 12 with her mother. Her passage into the country was traumatic. She was assaulted and separated from her mother who ended up being sent back to Mexico. Marisa was taken in by relatives who looked after her well, but the memories of the passage always haunted her. The only comfort she could ever find was in food. She would eat dinner with the family, then retire to her room and eat whatever she had been able to hoard from the pantry, from school, and even from the trash. Her weight kept increasing and her family teased her about her developing body. Marisa was horrified and ashamed, but would just drown her tears in food. It wasn't until age 19 when she enrolled in a community college that she saw a poster offering group treatment for emotional eating that she was able to share with anyone the shame and horror she felt about her BED.

3 WHY ME? WHAT CAUSES BED?

If you are hoping for a simple answer to this question, you will be disappointed. Like so many conditions, BED is caused by a combination of genetic/biological and environmental factors. In fact, there are most likely differences in the causes across people—no two people's BED is exactly alike—which underscores why it is so important that we have a range of treatments from which to chose. One size definitely does not fit all when it comes to treatment of BED.

What doesn't cause BED? BED is very misunderstood. No one chooses to have BED. No one chooses to be unable to control their eating. Every person with BED whom I have ever met or treated has unequivocally wished that they could control their appetite. Choice does however play a role in recovery.

Genetics. Yes, genes play a role! We know that BED runs in families. Traits can run in families for two reasons: 1) because of modeling behaviors (i.e., watching others eat emotionally or binge); and 2) because of genetic factors. Most often, it is a combination of both. Studies of thousands of twins can actually help us disentangle the extent to which genetic factors contribute to traits running in families. Twin studies of BED tell us that somewhere between 40-60% of liability to developing BED is due to genetic factors. We have not yet identified the precise genes that influence the disorder, but our models predict that there will be hundreds of genes involved and that some of those genes might also influence body weight regulation.

That does NOT mean that genes are destiny. In fact, quite the opposite is true. You can probably have a strong genetic predisposition for BED and never develop the disorder if your environment isn't conducive to binge eating. As an extreme example, if you live on a remote island where all you have available to eat is fresh fruit and vegetables and the fish that you catch yourself, you might never develop the disorder. But, if you move to Main Street, USA and live close to any number of fast food restaurants, where heavily processed food is cheaper than fruits and vegetables, soft drinks are cheaper than milk, and everything is supersized, then those genes just might be more likely to be expressed and manifest in BED.

Neurobiology. Mice, rats, and even fruit flies are helping scientists to identify parts of the brain and pathways in the brain that control all aspects of appetite and eating including: what starts an eating episode, what stops an eating episode, what makes eating go on and on even when full, and what makes you not eat when you are hungry and food is available. These are all factors that go into regulating eating, and BED is of course an example of completely dysregulated eating. Many neurotransmitters (compounds that assist with signaling) like dopamine, serotonin, gamma-aminobutyric acid (GABA), and opioids seem to play interlocking roles in these processes. Several areas of the brain that may be implicated in BED deal with the experience of reward (responding to what feels good, tastes good, etc.), impulsivity (acting before thinking), emotion, and the experience of eating.

The gastrointestinal system (aka the gut). Gut hormones and peptides may also play a role in BED. It is not just our brain that signals when we are hungry and full. In fact, our stomach plays a very important role in signaling when to start eating and when to stop. If you have ever heard your stomach growl that is a very audible signal that you are hungry! Much subtler messages are being sent to your brain by your stomach, egging it on to get to the cafeteria for lunch or to grab something from the vending machine fast. Some of the major players are leptin (involved in signaling fullness) and ghrelin (involved in signaling hunger). But there are many more subtle biological signals and probably many that have yet to be discovered.

The environment. We could never have predicted our current toxic food environment. In fact, our environment is tailor-made to interrupt every appetite regulatory mechanism that we have evolved to have. Food cues everywhere (you can't even buy books or shoes without encountering food for sale these days), 48-ounce sodas, price structures that support unhealthy food choices, food advertising aimed at children, high-fructose corn syrup, additives and dyes, preservatives, and unpronounceable ingredients have all taken us so far away from healthful and mindful eating.

We have evolved to eat during times of plenty and survive on very little during times of famine. The food environment has changed very rapidly—more rapidly than any changes to our biology could take place. For most of us, the famine never comes yet we keep stockpiling as if it were just around the corner. The food and beverage industries contend that we have a choice regarding whether we want to eat the type and quantities of food they are marketing—but our biology overrides our will. Just like it's hard not to blink when someone flicks their fingers near your eye, it's hard to say "No" to food in today's environment. Industries spend billions trying to figure out how to get you to engage in as much hand-to-mouth feeding as you can...and to ensure that you come back for more. Our biological ability to say, "Stop!" pales in comparison.

This combination of biological and environmental factors creates a perfect storm for the development of BED. It's not that BED is new; in fact it was recognized in the scientific literature in the 1950s, but the circumstances for developing the disorder have become more conducive and recognition has improved.

Jack

Jack was a trained lawyer who was serving as a state senator in a Southern state. He was a true public servant and would do anything for his constituents. Jack came from a farming community and was raised on hearty Southern food that had been necessary to replace all of the energy that his family expended working in the fields from dawn to dusk. To him, Southern food was a warm reminder of all that was home. His parents had both passed, and the farm was sold to build a highway, but the memories lived on in food. As Jack traveled around the region, people would invite him in for meals. He had a reputation of loving a home-cooked meal and everyone knew he had a weak spot for shrimp and grits—and not the modern low-fat kind.

Jack knew his waistline was expanding. His doctor reminded him of that every time she took his blood pressure. But taking away his favorite foods was like losing his home and parents all over again. After his wife passed, Jack couldn't bring himself to cook, so he ate out almost every night. He would "be good" and only eat half of the serving at the restaurant, but he ripped into the doggie bag soon after getting back home, which would invariably jumpstart a binge. He'd finish the rest of the meal, then head to the cupboards for anything else he could find. Salty, sweet, he didn't care, and he often alternated back and forth. The food just wiped out the pain, if only for a short time.

What Jack didn't realize was how sad and lonely he was. He missed his family; he missed his home; and he desperately missed his wife. He loved serving his people, but aside from the food they fed him, the relationship was one-directional: it was always Jack helping them. No one realized how badly Jack could use some help and support of his own.

4 BED AND WEIGHT STIGMA

Chunky monkey, thunder thighs, bubble butt, balloon bottom…I was called every insulting name you can in high school. When they hurled the insults at me I was determined not to eat so that they couldn't call me those things any more—so I skipped lunch at school every day. By the time I got home around 3:30, I was famished. My mom didn't get home from work until after 5:00, so I had a whole hour and a half by myself. I would eat my way through whatever I could find. Sometimes I had to run to the store to replace the food before my mom got home so she wouldn't miss it. After I binged I would just lock myself in my room with my headphones on. Mom thought I was doing my homework, but I was just bawling in disgust with myself.
- Lisa, diagnosed with BED at age 36

Many people with BED have been put through the wringer of humiliation both as children and as adults. This is most common with those who are large, but people with BED of all sizes report teasing, bullying, and discrimination. These sorts of experiences are often at the root of cycles of dieting and binge eating that become part of an entrenched BED pattern. It is for this reason that many people with BED believe that weight loss should not be an explicit criterion for recovery from BED and that the main focus should be on abstinence from, or reduction in, binge eating.

The diet-binge cycle. We know that dieting or food restriction precedes binge eating in many cases. Many people with BED report going through periods of strict dieting before their binge eating set in. A smaller percentage of individuals say that the binge eating started first and that they seem to have been born with voracious appetites and no "full" indicator. If we focus on those who reported dieting first, what we see are patterns that vacillate back and forth between restricting and then rebound binge eating. It is almost as if the body says, "I can't take it anymore!" and then breaks through the diet with a binge. Even people without BED know that if you miss a meal and are really hungry, you eat faster and more than if you have regularly spaced meals and never get to that point of being famished. One theory claims that this repeated cycle of restricting and binge eating basically erases any inborn signals you might have that tell you when you are hungry or full. Typically, these signals come primarily from the stomach (the gut) and the brain, and they talk to each other. We also know that fat cells play a role in this signaling, but we know less about how fat itself interferes with the communication between the gut and the brain. The important point is that there is complete communication breakdown in BED. The signals to start eating seem to always be on, and the checkered flag just never comes out.

In no way are we saying to ignore health problems that are associated with being overweight or obese. What advocates do argue about is whether weight loss should be an explicit goal of BED treatment. They contend that the pressure to lose weight just catapults individuals back into that terrible cycle of restriction and binge eating. A more measured approach is to concentrate treatment on abstinence from or reduction of binge eating. That means not focusing on the number on the scale but rather on healthful regular eating, physical activity that you enjoy, and other health-maintaining behaviors. With that focus, you are likely to see positive changes in cholesterol, blood pressure, and other metabolic indicators even before you see any changes in the number on the scale. After all, these are very important indices of health, and a focus on them is infinitely more helpful than a focus on what you weigh.

Dealing with weight stigma. Individuals with BED who are large may still be the butt of sick jokes, inappropriate comments, disapproving glances, name calling, and frank discrimination even well into adulthood. Humans are fascinated and threatened by extremes, which is one of the reasons that they feel compelled to comment on or denigrate those who fall outside of the average. Large patients with whom I have worked claim that people will come up to them in the checkout line and comment disapprovingly on what they have in their cart. One patient was getting an ice cream with her daughter and the man behind her in line asked if she thought she *really* needed that! Being turned down for jobs, denied rental apartments, getting lower grades, and being less likely to find a partner are all related to discrimination against people of size. Episodes of weight stigma are commonly cited as powerful triggers for binge eating.

Even health care professionals are biased against large patients. Many prefer not to work with large patients, and most feel incompetent when it comes to dealing effectively with their health and weight management. "Go on a diet" is a common recommendation; yet we all know (or should know by now) that diets don't work and are perhaps the best way to gain weight—and for someone with BED, diets are the best way to trigger a binge.

An effective way to deal with weight stigma is to become involved with social network communities that counter weight stigma and call discrimination out when they see it. The kind of acceptance offered by these communities is central to defusing the power that discrimination has to influence your behavior and your feelings about yourself. Several resources included in the appendix serve this role for countless men and women with BED who struggle with weight stigmatization.

5 PSYCHOLOGICAL TREATMENTS FOR BED

The single most important message from this handbook is that BED is treatable. Many people can get their BED under complete control and become abstinent from binge eating (meaning they no longer binge at all). Others can experience drastic reductions in how often they binge. The trick is finding the treatment that is right for you and sticking with it. Sometimes people are afraid to give up the binge eating. Food can be a security blanket. Patients might worry about what could fill the void that binge eating currently fills. What will take its place? What will I do when I am stressed? Bored? Lonely? Many people say that food has become their best friend. Whereas other friends might not be there in their times of need, food is always available and waiting to comfort them. The problem is that food is also their worst enemy. Even though it might seem like a friend in the short-term, by later that evening or the next morning, it has transformed into an enemy.

The next two sections discuss psychotherapy and medication for BED. Work with your physician or health care provider to determine which treatment or treatments are best for you. When looking for a therapist to treat your BED, seek out someone with experience in treating eating disorders and, if possible, BED. Many of the therapy approaches to treating BED are common across eating disorders, so experience with anorexia nervosa or bulimia nervosa is also valuable. If weight is an issue for you, you'll want to make sure that you and your therapist are aligned in how you are going to approach the issue of weight in your treatment. It is your right to bring this question up.

How long treatment takes varies by person. For some people, a brief course of psychotherapy (around 20 sessions or fewer) is enough; for others, it takes longer. We do not yet have a way of predicting how long treatment will take for any given person. The critical first step is to get a comprehensive professional assessment.

Assessment. In the best of all possible worlds, an assessment for BED would include a physical examination by an MD, a thorough psychological evaluation by a psychologist or other health care professional, and a nutritional evaluation by a registered dietitian. Of course, not everyone has access to this array of practitioners, nor will everyone's insurance cover this kind of an evaluation. The physician will review your health history and your medications, check your vital signs, conduct a physical exam, and take blood to do a range of tests. In the psychological evaluation, you will be asked extensive questions about your eating behaviors and history and about other problems you may have faced, such as depression, anxiety, and alcohol or drug use or abuse—and how they might be related to your BED. The dietitian will ask about your weekly and daily eating habits and get a sense of what your diet and patterns of eating are like (both binge and non-binge episodes). If you haven't spoken about these things before, it might be a little hard to have these conversations frankly. But the more honest you can be, the better your clinicians will be able to tailor a treatment to your needs. By practicing radical honesty, you will help them design the treatment that will fit you best.

Self-help. Many people find that picking up a self-help book for BED (or an online program or app) can go a long way toward getting their binge-eating behavior under control. Some self-help approaches are entirely self-help, whereas others may be guided by a coach or therapist or include a component with input from a health care professional. Self-help approaches often apply techniques that are distilled from types of psychotherapy that have been found to be helpful for people with BED such as cognitive-behavioral therapy (CBT) or mindfulness (more on these later). These approaches help you to monitor patterns in your eating and binge eating, identify triggers or cues for binge eating, and find alternatives to binge eating to manage your emotions. For some people, just seeing the patterns of their binge eating behaviors goes a long way toward figuring out how to break the cycle. What seemed like an uncontrollable situation becomes more manageable when you understand what the patterns are and are able to predict and preempt them.

Cognitive-behavioral therapy (CBT). CBT has the most empirical evidence behind it for the treatment of BED. Several clinical trials have shown that between half and two-thirds of individuals who undergo a course of CBT are either abstinent from binge eating or show significant reductions in how often they binge. CBT uses well-documented techniques like self-monitoring (keeping track of your eating, your binge eating, your sleep, your moods, etc. in order to uncover patterns), thought and mood recognition (understanding what the thoughts and feelings are that trigger binges), cue recognition (identifying other triggers in the environment like conflict, stress, aggravation, and frustration), alternative reinforcers (finding other ways to soothe or reward yourself aside from food), chaining (unpacking what the sequence of events, thoughts, and feelings are that lead up to a binge), thought restructuring (learning how to transform your thinking to support healthy behavior), and relapse prevention (how to keep it all from happening again). CBT is an active treatment. Your therapist works with you to learn and practice all of these techniques, and you develop a game plan for staying healthy after therapy ends.

Interpersonal psychotherapy (IPT). IPT focuses more on the interpersonal factors that contribute to binge eating. Many people find that various forms of human interactions (or the lack thereof) play a role in their BED. IPT explores how interactions keep BED alive and works to address the interpersonal problems directly. Whereas CBT is very focused on the symptoms of BED, IPT looks more at the context in which BED occurs. Some patients claim that CBT is an important starting point to get the symptoms under control, but that they benefitted from interpersonal approaches after that. The lesson there is that sometimes more than one approach, perhaps in sequence, might work for you.

Mindfulness. Mindfulness approaches to BED focus on training individuals in mindfulness meditation and guided mindfulness practices. The goal is to use these techniques to help people with BED manage their responses to strong emotions, make conscious rather than impulsive food choices, re-learn how to recognize hunger and fullness signals, and improve self-acceptance. Mindfulness helps patients to focus more on internal cues related to hunger and fullness rather than external cues (emotions, smells, other people, the presence of tempting foods etc.). This approach also helps retrain people in how to be more aware of their hunger and distinguishing between needing and wanting food (hunger versus pleasure).

Other psychotherapies. Other forms of psychotherapy that have been less extensively tested, but have shown some promise in the treatment of BED, include Dialectical Behavioral Therapy (DBT), Appetite Awareness Training (AAT), and Acceptance and Commitment Therapy (ACT). If you find a therapist who practices one of these types of therapy, make sure that he or she has experience working with eating disorders, and preferably BED.

An important note about psychotherapy. The goal of psychotherapy for BED is to stop or reduce binge eating. Many patients who are overweight enter therapy for BED thinking that weight loss is the goal or believing that if you stop binge eating, you will immediately lose weight. This is not the case. Whereas these therapies can be very effective in decreasing binge eating, they are not weight-loss treatments. In fact, many people find that they do not lose weight, even after becoming abstinent from binge eating. That is not a treatment failure! It is very important to focus on getting the binge eating under control. You can then work with your therapist on how and whether you want to tackle weight management. If you start going on diets and restricting during therapy, you can undo all of your hard work and find yourself right back in the middle of the diet-binge cycle.

The body craves regularity. Regardless of the therapeutic approach that you choose, one piece of recovery that you can start working on yourself is developing and maintaining a regular schedule in your life. This means eating your meals and snacks at predictable and regular times every day, going to sleep and waking up around the same time every day (weekdays and weekends as much as possible), and engaging in regular physical activity. People with BED often find that these systems are terribly out of whack, which does not respect the body's need for predictability. Establishing and maintaining regular routines is one of the best ways to launch recovery from BED.

6 MEDICATION TREATMENTS FOR BED

Medications can also play an important role in the treatment of BED. That being said, all of the medications that have been tested for BED have been "borrowed" from other illnesses like depression, epilepsy, or attention deficit hyperactivity disorder. That does not mean that BED is a variant of those illnesses, but rather that the biological systems that those medications act on also have an effect on binge eating.

Additionally, it is important to recognize that most of the clinical treatment trials for BED have been short term and they have not yet studied long-term outcomes. What that means is that we do not know how long the improvements in binge eating last or if people are likely to relapse a year or two after treatment. What we do know is that medication can be effective in the short term and it can also be a way to get the symptoms of binge eating under control so that you are in a better place to benefit from psychotherapy. Several different classes of medications have been tested for BED. Several of them have been used "off-label", meaning that they are typically prescribed for another condition, seem to work for BED, but have not been officially approved by the Food and Drug Administration (FDA) to treat BED. In January 2015, the FDA approved Vyvanse (an amphetamine) for the treatment of BED. This is only the second drug ever to have been approved for the treatment of any eating disorder—the first was fluoxetine (Prozac) for bulimia nervosa. Ask your physician if any of the medications discussed below might be appropriate for you.

Antidepressants. Several antidepressant medications have been tested in the treatment of BED including fluoxetine, fluvoxamine, sertraline, escitalopram, citalopram, duloxetine, bupropion, desipramine, and imipramine. The most commonly studied medication is fluoxetine, which has shown some short-term benefits in reducing binge eating in some but not all studies. In general, antidepressants may increase the speed with which binge eating declines, may help with depression, and may decrease binge eating; however, their results tend to be neither dramatic nor long lived.

Anticonvulsants. Medications typically used to treat conditions such as epilepsy have also been tested in BED. Topiramate has been the most widely studied and has been shown to be associated with remission from binge eating, the speed with which binge eating decreases, and weight loss. However, some patients find the side effects of topiramate, especially cognitive side effects, difficult to tolerate. Studies of two other anticonvulsants, zonisamide and lamotrigine, provided less convincing results, although lamotrigine did improve metabolic parameters, such as glucose and triglyceride levels, commonly associated with obesity and type 2 diabetes.

Anti-obesity medications. Given that many individuals with BED are also overweight, it was sensible to test medications designed to treat obesity. Unfortunately, several of the medications that were tested have been subsequently removed from the market due to dangerous side effects and will not be discussed here. One remaining medication, orlistat, has not shown consistent benefits in reducing binge eating.

Psychostimulants and drugs used to treat attention deficit activity disorder (ADHD). Psychostimulants are most commonly used to treat ADHD, and one, lisdexamfetamine (Vyvanse), is now indicated for the treatment of BED by the FDA. In clinical trials, patients taking Vyvanse reported fewer binge days per week than patients who were given a placebo (inactive pill). Anecdotal reports from patients reveal that the medication reduces their drive to binge, allowing them to control their appetite. As it is an amphetamine, there is concern for addiction and cardiovascular (e.g., blood pressure, stroke) and psychiatric side effects. Vyvanse is a Schedule II controlled substance meaning that it has a high potential for abuse and may lead to psychological or physical dependence. Therefore, like any medication, it should only be used as prescribed.

Atomoxetine, a norepinephrine uptake inhibitor also used to treat ADHD, has also been associated with greater binge remission, reduction in binge frequency, and weight loss.

Other medications. Other medications that have been tried for BED treatment include memantine, a drug used to treat symptoms of Alzheimer's disease, which was associated with a significant reduction in binge eating but no change in weight; chromium picolinate, a dietary supplement that was not superior to placebo in one small clinical trial; and medications used to treat addictions, namely acamprosate and naloxone. Results of these trials are not yet sufficiently robust to recommend these drugs for the treatment of BED.

Things to keep in mind when treating BED with medications. As with any medication, potential side effects and interactions with other drugs should be carefully considered before prescribing them for BED. It is also critical to remember that medication alone has not been shown to be an effective long-term treatment for BED. Few long-term trials have been conducted. We also do not yet know the optimal duration of drug treatment. Finally, we know next to nothing about how medication treatment for BED would differ between men and women or across various races and ethnicities. It remains important for all patients with BED to learn behavioral and emotion regulation strategies to help develop confidence in one's ability to control binge eating over time.

CLOSING REMARKS

BED is treatable, and there is a vibrant community of people who have dealt with BED themselves or in their family members who are ready to support you. Reach out! Ask for help! Don't try to do it alone! Whether you try self-help approaches first or opt for therapy or medication, there is a range of options for you to try. Importantly, do not get discouraged. Just like any medical condition, sometimes the first thing you try doesn't work. Your doctor might need to try several medications before she or he finds the right one for you—the same holds for BED. In fact, let's say that CBT didn't work for you when you were 25. That doesn't mean that it won't work when you are 30. You might be in a different space and one that is more amenable to that approach. Typically it takes several years (sometimes decades) for BED to get established, so you can't expect that it will go away completely in four weeks! Habits are difficult to change, and you may need time and support to become well. The next section provides a number of resources, from support communities to books and articles about BED. Becoming informed and involved are two ways to engage in the recovery process. Be dogged in your search for resources and support, and never lose hope!

APPENDIX:
WHERE TO FIND HELP AND SUPPORT

For more in-depth treatment of BED, see:

Bulik, C.M. (2009) *Crave: Why You Binge and How to Stop.* New York: Walker.
Bulik, C.M. (2013) *Midlife Eating Disorders: Your Journey to Recovery.* New York: Walker.

General Resources

National Institute of Mental Health (NIMH)
The National Institute of Mental Health (NIMH) offers information and services for those in need. The NIMH provides information to help people better understand mental health, mental disorders, and behavioral problems. Referrals are not provided.

Contact information:
6001 Executive Boulevard
Room 8184, MSC 9663
Bethesda, MD 20892-9663 USA
Telephone: 1-866-615-6464 toll-free or (301) 443-4513
Fax: (301) 443-4279
E-mail: nimhinfo@nih.gov
Website: www.nimh.nih.gov
Facebook: National Institute of Mental Health
Twitter: @NIMHgov

Advocacy Groups

Binge Eating Disorder Association (BEDA)
From the BEDA website: "Founded in 2008, the Binge Eating Disorder Association (BEDA) is a national organization focused on providing leadership, recognition, prevention, and treatment of BED and associated weight stigma. Through outreach, education and advocacy, BEDA will facilitate increased awareness and proper diagnosis of BED, and promote excellence in care for those who live with, and those who treat, binge eating disorder and its associated conditions. BEDA is committed to promoting cultural acceptance of, and respect for, the natural diversity of sizes, as well as promoting a goal of improved health, which may or may not include weight change."

Contact information:
Binge Eating Disorder Association, Inc.
550M Ritchie Hwy, #271
Severna Park, MD 21146 USA
Telephone: 443-597-0066
Fax: 410-544-4640
E-mail: info@bedaonline.com
Website: www.bedaonline.com
Facebook: Binge Eating Disorder Association
Twitter: @BEDAorg

BingeBehavior.com
From the BingeBehavior.com website: "BingeBehavior.com is a website designed to support people with BED, impulse control disorders (Body Focused Repetitive Behaviors – BRFBs), and who battle weight bias and stigma. The purpose of BingeBehavior.com is to alleviate stigma and shame through information, resource identification and advocacy. The work of BingeBehavior.com is two fold: to aggregate information supporting people with BED/BFRBs **AND** to advocate for the end of weight bias and stigma and related injustice in size diversity. Mental health challenges and size discrimination are by their nature isolating but with persistence, we can challenge the idea that seeking help or that speaking up for one's rights is in any way shaming. IT IS INDEED A BOLD AND IMPORTANT PURSUIT!"

Contact information:
Telephone: 202-415-6987
E-mail: admin@bingebehavior.com
Website: www.bingebehavior.com

Facebook: BingeBehavior.com
Twitter: @BingeBehavior
G+: BingeBehavior.com
Pinterest: BingeBehavior.com

Eating Disorders Coalition (EDC)
The Eating Disorders Coalition's mission is "...to advance the federal recognition of eating disorders as a public health priority." This is the group that lobbies on Capitol Hill in order to improve funding for research, treatment, and education of eating disorders. They also work towards better insurance coverage and the recognition of eating disorders as serious illnesses worthy of adequate insurance coverage.

Contact information:
Eating Disorders Coalition
611 Pennsylvania Avenue SE #423
Washington, DC 20003-4303 USA
Telephone: 202-543-9570
Website: www.eatingdisorderscoalition.org
Facebook: Eating Disorders Coalition for Research, Policy & Action
Twitter: @EDCoalition

National Eating Disorders Association (NEDA)
From the NEDA website: "The National Eating Disorders Association (NEDA) is the largest not-for-profit organization in the United States working to prevent eating disorders and provide treatment referrals to those suffering from anorexia, bulimia, and BED and those concerned with body image and weight issues."

Contact information:
603 Stewart St.
Suite 803
Seattle, WA 98101 USA
Business Office: (206) 382-3587
Toll-free Information and Referral Helpline: (800) 931-2237
Email: info@NationalEatingDisorders.org
Website: www.nationaleatingdisorders.org
Facebook: National Eating Disorders Association
Twitter: @NEDAstaff

Professional Organization

Academy for Eating Disorders (AED)
From the AED website: "The Academy for Eating Disorders (AED) is a global, multidisciplinary professional organization that provides cutting-edge professional training and education, inspires new developments in eating disorders research, prevention, and clinical treatments, and is the international source for state-of-the-art information in the field of eating disorders. AED strives for both education and practicality as it grows along with the number of eating disorder cases it sees every year. Advocacy and understanding are the foundations of this well-respected academy."

Contact information:
Academy for Eating Disorders
AED Headquarters
12100 Sunset Hills Road
Suite 130
Reston, VA 20190
E-mail: info@aedweb.org
Telephone: 847-498-4274
Facsimile: 847-480-9282
Website: www.aedweb.org
Facebook: Academy for Eating Disorders
Twitter: @aedweb

ABOUT THE AUTHOR

Cynthia M. Bulik, Ph.D., FAED, is Distinguished Professor of Eating Disorders in the Department of Psychiatry in the School of Medicine at the University of North Carolina at Chapel Hill, where she is also Professor of Nutrition in the Gillings School of Global Public Health, and founding director of the UNC Center of Excellence for Eating Disorders, and co-director of the UNC Center for Psychiatric Genomics. She is also Professor in the Department of Medical Epidemiology and Biostatistics at the Karolinska Institutet, in Stockholm, Sweden.

Dr. Bulik, a clinical psychologist, has been conducting research and treating individuals with eating disorders since 1982. She received her BA from the University of Notre Dame and her MA and PhD from the University of California, Berkeley. She completed internships and post-doctoral fellowships at the Western Psychiatric Institute and Clinic in Pittsburgh, PA and developed treatment services for eating disorders both in New Zealand and in the United States. Her research includes treatment, laboratory, epidemiological, twin, and molecular genetic studies of eating disorders and body weight regulation. She has active research collaborations throughout the United States and in over twenty countries around the world. She has published over 480 papers and chapters on eating disorders and is author of several books including *Crave: Why You Binge Eat and How to Stop*, *The Woman in the Mirror*, and *Midlife Eating Disorders: Your Journey to Recovery*.

Dr. Bulik is a recipient of numerous awards and is past president of the Academy for Eating Disorders, past Vice President of the Eating Disorders Coalition, past Associate Editor of the International Journal of Eating Disorders, Founding Chair of the Scientific Advisory Council of the Binge Eating Disorder Association, and a member of the Scientific Advisory Committee of the Global Foundation for Eating Disorders.

Dr. Bulik is passionate about translating science for the public. Her television appearances include the Today Show, Good Morning America, CBS This Morning, CNN Morning, Katie, Dr. Oz, Dr. Phil, and Rachael Ray. She has been featured in the *New York Times*, the *Washington Post*, *USA Today*, *Newsweek*, *Time*, and the *US News and World Report*. Dr. Bulik holds the first endowed professorship in eating disorders in the United States. She balances her work life by being by being happily married, the mother of three, a gold medalist in ice dancing, and an avid ballroom dancer. Read more at http://cynthiabulik.com.

Made in the USA
Middletown, DE
30 July 2020